STEPPING OUT OF DEPRESSION

Fresh Hope for Women Who Hurt

Jamie Meyer

Acknowledgements

This undertaking would not have been possible without the loving support of my husband, Allen. You are my rock and my encourager. Thank you for always believing in me and giving me the time and space to write.

Thank you to my children, Matthew, Kelly, and Kevin, who allowed me to use their stories in the book. You've taught me more than you could possibly know. I thank God for the privilege of being your mother. You were beside me when I had the brain tumor and there through my battle with depression. Even though you are now scattered around the country, you are always close in heart.

For providing encouraging feedback when I had doubts about the manuscript God laid on my heart, I want to thank Julie, Kylee, and Carol. Your encouragement was music to my ears and a confirmation that these words needed to be written down and placed in the hands of women who hurt.

To the courageous women who sat down with me

over coffee to share their stories: your words were such a blessing. It gave me great comfort to know that other women have been in my shoes, experiencing the entire range of emotions that accompany depression, and have been victorious over the disease. Thank you for your time and, most of all, your honesty.

A book would not be complete without someone to proofread and edit. Thank you, Michelle Nash, for providing your expertise. Your English students are blessed to have you for a teacher.

And for the beautiful book cover, I want to thank my friend and fellow life group member, Angie Johnson. I am amazed at the artistic skill with which God has blessed you. Thank you for using your gifts to create this work of art.

To my self-publisher, Xulon Press, for your support and guidance throughout the publishing process. It has been a joy to work with you and to know that we share the same values and love for God. Thank you for seeing this labor of love through to completion.

Contents

INTRODUCTION

Depression invites many questions: *What causes it? How do we treat it? Is medication necessary? How long before I feel like myself again?* Such questions are normal and expected when you are in the grip of depression. So how should you go about finding answers when even doctors have difficulty pinpointing the cause of a person's depression? This book will help you find the answers as you journey through the avenues of medicine, counseling therapy, and spirituality.

Depression has been described as everything from a physical illness to a spiritual problem to a disease. The disorder is not well understood because there is still much we don't know about the workings of the brain. Psychiatrists and researchers know antidepressant medications work, but they're not entirely sure how. Complicating the diagnosis are various factors that enter into the depression equation: life situations, physical illness or disability, losses of various kinds, emotional setbacks, and relational issues.

This painful disease disorients those who suffer in its grip, causing them to temporarily lose their way through life. I know; I've been there. When I traveled through depression, it felt like my life had derailed. I found myself alone, uncoupled and directionless, wondering where to turn. How does one go about literally getting "back on track," back to what is normal and familiar?

Alongside the disorientation of depression is the confusion of muddled thinking and mixed-up emotions. Hopelessness and the loss of interest in life can lead to the brink of decisions not based in reality. Concentration is difficult. Decision-making, whether at work or at home, becomes a consuming task. Emotions cloud everything, taking control rather than our being in control of them.

Depression cuts to the very core of who we are — our physical, mental, emotional, relational, and spiritual selves. Discussions of depression often address these first four attributes in detail but tend to overlook the latter. A book that addresses the spiritual impact of depression on women is needed in today's culture. There is a stigma in our society toward those with depression and mental illness and, sadly, this stigma is carried into the church. Our churches should be healing communities where people suffering from depression can find acceptance, support, and understanding. Unfortunately, that is not always the case.

There is an unwritten expectation in churches that Christians should look happy and meet certain standards of grooming on Sunday mornings. For those suffering from depression, it is especially difficult to put on a cheerful smile, let alone get dressed and perform the very minimum in personal hygiene. Clothes remain neatly hung in closets or tossed on the floor. Make-up and hairbrushes sit untouched in bathroom drawers.

In many ways, clothing and make-up are the least of our concerns. They take a backseat to a lack of energy which, at the very minimum, is required to get one's self out of bed. Few people understand this. It creates emotional pain for those who suffer, and leaves loved ones and church family confused. What begins as curious concern about a person's depression turns into disappointment as absences are noted week after week.

Let me clarify up front that I am not talking about a stretch of "blue" days or PMS. I am writing to those of you with moderate to severe depression for whom prayer and Bible study have been unable to bring about full recovery. Both significantly add to the cure, but by themselves are not the solution. Depression can be all-consuming and, as such, requires medical care and often counseling. It's no wonder that such a complicated disease is so misunderstood.

Many books on depression, while going into great detail about causes and cures, are not likely to be read by those experiencing depression. Concentration is limited and numerous pages can seem overwhelming. My desire in writing this book is to give you information in small bites—brief chapters you can turn to that will address your immediate concerns.

Feel free to skip around as your needs and interests require. You may need someone to read chapters to you. Don't feel ashamed that reading is exhausting at this stage in your depression. Many of us have experienced the same struggle.

My own journey through depression was unique. Yours will be too. I went through a serious medical condition a year before I was diagnosed with clinical depression; you may have experienced a number of losses or set-backs. I was in perimenopause; you may be postpartum. Whatever our individual histories, depression should be taken seriously and treated with respect.

My prayer for you is that you will come to a place of acceptance that, for reasons known only to Him, God has allowed depression in your life. I am a firm believer in Romans 8:28, that if we belong to Him, he will cause all things to work together for our good and (I might add) for His glory. It's hard to see right now how any good can come from your depression, but it will. There will be growth in your own life and an impact on the lives of those around you—your spouse, children, co-workers, friends, extended family, and church members.

Right now you may feel as though you're a burden to all of them. It's okay to be needy, since it allows others to love and serve you in ways they could not do otherwise. God designed us for fellowship, and sometimes that involves entering into the fellowship of Christ's sufferings as Paul says in Phillipians 3:10.

This is just one part of the mystery surrounding depression. Whether you sense it or not, loved ones are suffering with you during your time of need. They care for you and feel helpless to help you.

I also pray that as you make this very individual journey through depression you can learn to rest in the loving arms of Jesus. One of the more discouraging aspects of depression is that it may cause you to feel separated from God. The emptiness you feel inside leaves you with the perception that you have nothing to offer God whether through prayer, worship, praise, or gratitude.

Much like a child, you feel dependent on everyone around you to meet your needs. This is a very self-focused, lonely feeling. I understand. I've been there. God loves you just the way you are. He wants you to feel His love, and He invites you to share your burden with Him rather than carrying it yourself. Rest in Him, dear one, take His yoke upon you. His burden is light (Matt. 11:28-30).

Depression can entail a long journey, but there is hope. I stepped out of the blackness of depression and I know you can to. Allow me to share this hope in the pages that follow. You will hear stories of several women who traveled the road of depression with God at their side. They often felt like giving up and giving in to the pain and suffering, but they persevered in God's strength. Will you join me now as we take this journey together?

Depression's Voice

I do not choose to be depressed
nor to lounge in hopelessness,
far from those I love, so kind,
a prisoner of my heart and mind.

I sleep too much. My bones are weak,
I long for health. I cannot sleep.
Can you not see my spirit bleak?

Don't laugh nor judge
my tormented state.
Don't think I choose this
as my fate.

Read to me God's Word of Truth
and pray that I will find my worth
In Him alone who knows my frame,
when all I know is dark and pain.

Until Christ restores me in His grace
And I can see His precious face,
To love and serve Him evermore.
This is all I ask Him for.

CHAPTER 1

DEBBIE'S STORY

What is happening to me? Debbie thought, her eyes wandering to the in-box on her desk. *I've never been this far behind at work. What will my supervisor think?* Such thoughts had come more frequently to Debbie over the past several weeks. It was a struggle to stay focused on all the projects her boss had asked her to do. Some days she felt overwhelmed, not knowing where to start when she sat down at her desk in the morning. It was so frustrating, this inability to concentrate on the work she needed to do.

Falling behind was out of character for Debbie. She prided herself on being conscientious and even perfectionistic about her job. Co-workers had commented on what a great team player she was, always willing to help when needed. Now she could barely keep her own head above water. She was surprised no one had said anything, but she did notice that her co-workers didn't stop by her desk quite as often to chat. *What is the matter with me? I'm going to lose my job if I don't pull myself together.*

Debbie's situation is not that uncommon for women who struggle with depression. An increasing sense of dread hangs over their head like a dark cloud. Will my boss criticize me for falling behind? Will my co-workers notice that I haven't been myself lately? Will I get fired for not doing my job as well as expected? As is often the case, a woman's ability to function on the job is impacted by depression. Yet there are issues outside of work as well.

What Debbie hadn't noticed were the subtle changes she was experiencing away from her job. Some nights she was so exhausted when she arrived home that she'd kick off her shoes and collapse on the couch. Sometimes she fell asleep, completely forgetting about supper. Her husband, David, usually home late, grumbled that nothing was on the table for dinner. *I'm under a lot of pressure at work*, Debbie reasoned.

Mornings were even worse. Debbie was finding it harder to climb out of bed and get ready for work. She blamed this on the change of seasons as it was definitely darker in the mornings. She would stand in front of the closet for several minutes, puzzling over what to wear. Once she had to laugh at herself for forgetting to put on earrings. Being scatterbrained was just a sign of aging, wasn't it?

It's possible that Debbie is experiencing depression. It could also be work pressures spilling over into her home life that makes it look like a depressive episode. If work stress is the culprit, Debbie's functioning will return to normal when the challenges resolve themselves. If the stress continues and Debbie is not able to keep a healthy balance outside of work, she's likely to spiral down into depression.

This is Debbie's story. Others, too, have a story to

tell, one of emotions and symptoms unique to them. You may be experiencing a time of confusion, suffering, and loss. Eventually you will ask yourself: *How do I know if what I'm experiencing is depression?* To put your mind at ease, let's first take a look at what is not depression.

Questions for reflection and discussion:

1) In what ways can you relate to Debbie's experience?

2) What steps can you take to reduce the stress level in your relationships? In the workplace? At home?

3) Debbie was experiencing a lot of anxiety both at work and at home. What does Philippians 4:6-7 instruct us to do when we feel anxious or stressed? What makes this hard for you to do?

CHAPTER 2

IS IT DEPRESSION OR JUST THE BLUES?

Depression is a word today's culture throws around far too casually. We might say the weather is depressing, or someone is depressing to be around. We use the word to express disappointment or discouragement about something; for example, "I'm so depressed that I can't go to the movie with you." If we are speaking in terms of mental health, *depression* is often used to mean something it's not, like "I'm feeling down." With so much confusion, let's begin our discussion by clarifying what is meant by the term and what is not depression.

Taber's Medical Dictionary defines *depression* as "a mental disorder marked by altered mood…nearly every day, (and) markedly diminished interest or pleasure in most or all activities."[1]

Alternatively, doctors use the term *adjustment disorder* to describe mental or social stress that impairs normal functioning and is short-term in nature. Symptoms are expected to resolve themselves once the stress is alleviated, such as in Debbie's situation.[2] An adjustment disorder, however, is not depression.

The most common cause of an adjustment disorder

is a situation that triggers a low mood. This may include a lack of sleep, a number of cloudy days, emotional stresses, or even the time of year. For instance, it's common for many women to feel a letdown after the Christmas holiday. The tree is taken down, ornaments are packed away, and the relatives have all gone home. All that remain are the leftovers in the refrigerator, food we surely don't need after a month of eating!

The low mood lifts when conditions change. Feeling more rested after a few good nights of sleep may help you be more alert and focused. Or just when you think you'll never see the sun again, it makes its appearance, lifting your mood if you are extra sensitive to gray days. And we know that holidays will come and go, bringing friends and loved ones for a brief visit before life returns to normal.

An adjustment disorder can also be caused by the side effects of medications. Such drugs may include steroids such as prednisone or cortisone, or medications to treat high blood pressure or heart conditions. Taking birth control pills can also be a factor, affecting many younger women.[3]

Infections and diseases can contribute to adjustment disorders. Those of us who have experienced a sinus infection are familiar with the facial pain and pressure that makes life miserable. As days turn into weeks, tiredness and discouragement settle in. Even after starting on an antibiotic, it can take several days for relief to arrive. Bladder and vaginal infections can be discouraging to women as well.

Diseases with constant or intermittent pain can also lead to feelings of discouragement. Most common are lupus, fibromyalgia, and arthritis. Many women suffer for months before an accurate diagnosis is made in these situations. Long waits with no answers for the pain simply adds to the emotional burden. While there is no cure for these diseases, women can work with their doctors to obtain the best possible treatment for their pain and reduce the likelihood of a serious depression.

There are also medical conditions or "syndromes" that can trigger depressive feelings. These include ulcers, rheumatoid arthritis, low blood sugar and diabetes, a low level of thyroid hormone, migraine headaches, or chronic fatigue syndrome.

Another trigger for feeling down can follow a major life change. If you've ever moved to a new community, had a baby, or been through major surgery, you know the uncomfortable feeling of waiting, whether for physical recovery or for new friendships to develop. Both patience and mood are tested during these times.

Another major life change is divorce or the death of a loved one. Inherent in such a loss is a normal grieving process. Elisabeth Kubler-Ross describes five stages of grief that most individuals experience as they heal from a major loss. These include denial, anger, bargaining, depression, and acceptance.[4] As time passes, grief will begin to resolve itself as life returns to a new normal.

And finally, there are spiritual causes for feeling blue. Some women are discouraged by their inability to connect with God in a meaningful way. I recall spending many years learning *about* God through sermons, Sunday school classes, and Bible studies. Growing in knowledge didn't seem to change my heart, leaving me feeling anxious and guilty.

Then one day a friend explained that Jesus wanted to have a close, personal relationship with me. His desire was to love and care for me like I loved and cared for my own children. This was a God I could relate to! So I said a simple prayer, asking Jesus to forgive my sins and fill me with His presence.

The changes I experienced after that day were gradual. I noticed my heart becoming more receptive to spiritual matters; bad habits were slowly transformed. Now I am no longer just learning about God. We have a heart-to-heart relationship where I feel free to talk to Him and listen as I read His Word, the Bible.

Perhaps you, too, have become dissatisfied with simply growing in knowledge through church teaching and Bible study. Perhaps you feel that your prayers are ineffective. Then I would encourage you to take a step of faith, as I did, to trust in the One who died for your sins. God loves you more than you can imagine and He wants you to experience an abundant, joy-filled life.

Refusing to forgive someone may also trigger a spiritual depression. When we make the choice to forgive, we receive God's power to release the other person from the bondage of our anger and resentment. This lifts the weight of unforgiveness from our heart.

And how often have we held on to sins that need to be acknowledged and confessed to God? With an attitude of love, the Holy Spirit prompts us with feelings of guilt to make us aware of our wayward thoughts and behaviors. This gives us the opportunity to ask for forgiveness, renewing our relationship with God.

Shame is another cause of spiritual despondency because it pulls our mood and self-esteem down. It's important to acknowledge here that shame is not from God. Our sin and shame were nailed to the cross with our Savior who died to release us from their power. If you are feeling down because of shameful thoughts, I encourage you to bring these to the Lord. Allow Him to remove them from your heart and mind, and replace them with His peace.

As we've seen, there are a number of reasons why you may be experiencing an adjustment disorder or the "blues." Identifying the cause is an important first step. This leads to recognition that what you're feeling is short-term, or may come and go in the case of a disease or medical condition. God will empower you to assume responsibility for your mood in these situations if you ask Him. Since our thought life impacts our feelings, if we learn to take "every thought captive to the obedience of Christ" (2 Cor. 10:5), we can begin to influence our feelings in a positive way.

But it takes more than positive thinking to battle an episode of depression. We want to turn our attention now to the symptoms and feelings associated with the dark demon known as major depression.

Questions for reflection and discussion:

1) How is feeling "down in the dumps" different from being depressed?

2) Can you identify anything in your life that may be contributing to an adjustment disorder?

3) Life change can be positive or negative depending on how we perceive the change. Have you recently experienced a major life change such as a divorce, death of a loved one, giving birth, moving, or children leaving (or returning) to the nest? Explain.

4) Since what we *think* strongly influences how we *feel*, what does it mean to "take every thought captive to the obedience of Christ" (2 Cor. 10:5)? You may want to look up this verse in other translations of the Bible for greater understanding.

CHAPTER 3

BLACK HOLES AND DEEP PITS

Depression can be a one-time event, or it can recur over the course of a person's lifetime. I have experienced both. My season-related depression, known as seasonal affective disorder (SAD), returns like clockwork once the hours of daylight start to wane in the fall. It often begins around the time daylight savings time ends, in September or October. In the spring (April or May), I find that my mood and energy level lift considerably.

I've also experienced major depression. Like Debbie, the first changes I noticed were in my energy level and feelings of self-worth. Although I sensed my mood spiraling downward, I was so distracted by the changes in our lives that I ignored what was happening.

Before the depression arrived, stressful events began to build one by one: we sold our home of eighteen years and built a new one; we moved twice in a three-month period; a college student lived with us for a school semester; and our daughter's fiancé broke off their engagement just six weeks before the wedding. Being a person who is sensitive to change, I nevertheless thought I was managing the stresses well. But the broken engagement was the last straw, so to speak, that sent me over the edge emotionally.

After the break-up, our daughter, Kelly, returned to college in Chicago. Getting her back on track was a relief for my husband, Allen, and me. I thought I was doing a good job holding our family together, but shortly after Kelly returned to school I fell into the pit of depression.

Normally one to feel a little less energy in the cold winter months, I was more lethargic than I could ever remember. I had difficulty getting out of bed on my days off from work and spent a good part of the day in my pajamas and robe. I didn't have the energy to shower and get dressed. Cooking and cleaning were the first home responsibilities to go. I just didn't feel like doing anything.

My mood slid slowly downward as I began to feel guilty about my inability to function normally. My mind flooded with negative thoughts, the most common one being "I just don't care." Listen as I share the experience of depression through the eyes of my journal:

Tears seem to come far too easily and I wonder: Will life ever be the same? I can't seem to handle any kind of frustration without anger or tears. So many things seem overwhelming to me right now. I realize I need to ask for help and not try to make everything my burden.

Two months into my depression Allen and I sought out the help of a psychiatrist. He was very caring and indeed diagnosed me with depression. I was given a low dose of antidepressant that would gradually be increased in strength over the course of six weeks.

I am cautiously hopeful. At this point I feel dead inside and am living to get through each day. I don't feel hopeful about the future nor do I have anything to look forward to. I desperately want the medicine to work because I don't know what to do next if it doesn't.

I find myself cycling up and down like a roller coaster. On good days I have the motivation and energy to do things, to get out of the house. On bad days I sit on the couch all day doing number puzzles, watching TV, or sleeping. On those days I feel guilty for being so unproductive and not being able to care for my home or others. It takes a lot of energy just to climb into the shower and wash my hair.

So that you might better relate to the experience of severe depression, here are several thoughts from my journal:

- *All my energy goes toward getting through each day. I can't think about the future.*
- *I have lots of guilt: for being lazy, self-focused, and lacking the energy or desire to care for others.*
- *My world has become very small.*
- *I focus inward and am not as aware of the people around me.*
- *The word "hope" holds no meaning. I feel that life will always be this way.*
- *I feel less human because of being isolated from other people.*
- *I've lost connection with God, partly because He seems distant and I feel all alone, but also because going to church and having fellowship with other Christians takes too much energy.*

I wonder how many people in the world walk around each day looking fine on the outside yet inside they are filled with anxiety and depression. I am wondering because I am one of them. I go to work. I laugh when others laugh. I can carry on a conversation—all of the things normal people do—yet no one can see the pain I feel inside. I feel so alone in my depression yet I wonder how many "walking wounded" are around me.

Eventually, I was forced to give up my part-time job. I could not meet the expectation to socialize outside of work. I didn't even have the emotional strength to attend a staff retreat out of state. Taking vacation hours several times over the two years of my depression led to feelings of unfairness among my co-workers.

My job performance was not up to expectations; not being able to concentrate, I started making mistakes. I finally decided to resign, taking the burden off me and my employer.

Slowly, gradually, I improved with the assistance of medication. To help me reach the point of feeling "normal" again, the psychiatrist added two other medications. One was an antidepressant and the other a mood stabilizer, the latter of which significantly decreased my mood swings.

In addition to the medications, I started seeing a psychologist for counseling. He helped me address the issues of pain and loss that likely triggered my depression. He also helped me understand the importance of self-care and not being so hard on myself when I needed to take time out to rest and recharge. The combination of counseling and medications seemed to speed up my recovery.

If you asked me today I would tell you that I'm still on the healing journey, gaining new insights into myself and learning how to cope with life's ups and downs. I've learned to accept that medication is a part of my life now, and that seeing a Christian counselor significantly improves my outlook and my ability to cope with life. When I get discouraged with the necessity for continued treatment, I remind myself that God uses doctors, medicines, and counselors to heal us from diseases. Utilizing these resources is an important part of the healing process.

My story may not be a reflection of your story, however, so let's hear from several Christian women who've also experienced the "valley of the shadow." You may find that you are walking in their footsteps.

Questions for reflection and discussion:

1) Make a list of all the negative thoughts you are currently experiencing. How might each of these affect your mood?

2) In what ways do you identify with the author's journal entries? Which phrases resonate with your experience of depression?

3) Do you see yourself as one of the "walking wounded?" What specific behaviors do you use to hide your depression from others?

CHAPTER 4

WALKING THEIR WALK

Cheryl, 56, is a nurse at our local hospital. She recently shared that her heart was filled with joy over her son's upcoming wedding. Her future daughter-in-law was delighted to have Cheryl's help in planning for the big event. The time went by quickly, filled with bridal showers, final fittings, and decorating for the reception. At last the big day arrived. Everyone looked beautiful; the wedding and reception flew by far too quickly. While a certain amount of let-down was to be expected, Cheryl noticed that as the weeks after the wedding wore on, she was feeling less and less like herself.

"I began to feel a lot of anxiety over making decisions," Cheryl recalled. "I couldn't decide what to cook for dinner or whether I should vacuum or not. I remember one week when I couldn't get out of my chair. It was like I was frozen. I couldn't talk about things. I just wanted to be left alone.

"It felt like being trapped in a room, trapped in myself," Cheryl continued. "I didn't want to be the way I was but I couldn't change it. I remember not being able to get my mind off myself. I'd beat myself up for thinking so selfishly. I felt sad that I wasn't able to enjoy my family and friends. I felt I was missing out, like being on the outside looking in."

Terri, 25, is a graduate student studying journalism. She describes many of the same feelings as Cheryl. "I feel sad most of the time when I'm depressed. Mostly it's just sad for no reason. It's not something specific you can point to that explains the sadness. And then there's the fatigue; I feel it all over my body. My whole body feels like an enormous weight. It takes so much effort to stand up, and my muscles are sore from being so anxious and tense.

"It's so embarrassing not to be able to take care of yourself," Terri goes on to say. "Not able to sleep properly, eat healthfully, or make sure you're taking regular showers and getting dressed like an ordinary person would. And then there are the eating issues. I'm sensitive to my body so when I eat poorly I feel extra sluggish. I crave chocolate or anything with sugar in it. Carbohydrates: bagels, pasta, comfort foods. It gives me an instant upper, something I need when I feel depressed, but then I crash and feel worse than before."

Jackie, 43, mentors a group of high school girls and helps care for her aging mother. Her depression was triggered by a painful event in her life. "After awhile I realized that what I was experiencing was not a normal up and down mood. The initial event was so shocking that I spent an entire week on the sofa. I couldn't function.

"I didn't feel like eating, cooking, cleaning, doing anything. It was like I'd fallen into the bottom of a well. At first you feel like you're drowning, then maybe you can get your head above water. When I began to crawl out, a painful thought would send me down again. Eventually I reached the ledge and realized I could look out over the wall.

"I felt so isolated and lonely," Jackie continued, "like the world was moving on without me. You don't connect with anything or anyone. It's like walking around in a fog, going through the motions but feeling disconnected from yourself. Did I know it was depression? Having never been around anybody with depression, I don't think I knew. My husband and I were just dealing with the painful issue, not recognizing [the depression] for what it was."

Three women. Three different, yet similar, experiences of severe depression. Do you hear it in their voices? Sad, lonely, unable to connect with others, trapped in a well or a room, frozen. Can you relate to any of them? Beginning with a stressful event or situation, how is it that one can end up with major depression? Let's look at what happens when a woman's equilibrium is disrupted and she loses mental and emotional balance.

Questions for reflection and discussion:

1) Of the three women discussed in the chapter, who do you most relate to and why?

2) Describe what it feels like to be disconnected from yourself and others when depressed?

CHAPTER 5

TIPPING THE SCALES

For the most part women are able to keep their lives in a semblance of balance. They work and take care of household responsibilities, drive children to places they need to go, and provide support and encouragement to their spouses. They may care for elderly parents, school-age children, or busy toddlers.

Whether consciously aware of it or not, we engage in healthful practices that balance our stress: we eat, sleep, relax, do things we find enjoyable, and spend time with family and friends. All of these are designed to relieve stress and keep the physical and emotional scales balanced.

In the field of medicine the word *homeostasis* means that the body is constantly adjusting to changes in the environment to maintain a state of internal balance. For instance, when you exercise, your body responds by breathing faster to deliver more oxygen to the muscles. When you touch a hot stove, the brain tells the muscles to pull your hand away. If you are nervous, the body responds by breathing deeper and becoming more alert, what is called the "fight or flight" response. God created our mind and body to continually work together to maintain this healthy balance.

Problems occur when something disrupts this balancing act. Chronic stress is a major upset to both one's emotional and physiological balance. It causes the body to release stress hormones that, if allowed to persist unchecked, can damage the body and negatively impact the brain. Important chemical messengers in the brain (called neurotransmitters) are depleted, which in turn impacts a woman's mood. Over time she becomes literally stressed-out, causing her emotional and physical health to be jeopardized. When this happens, depression can occur.

Certain situations can also upset one's physical and emotional balance. Ongoing relationship difficulties can impact feelings of self-worth. Worsening medical conditions and the discouragement associated with them can tip a woman over the edge. So can spiritual confusion and negative thinking.

So why do some people get discouraged and others, depressed? I believe the primary difference is in how they perceive the distress. Let's say that two women are recent empty-nesters. Initially, both are sad to see their children leave home. This is an understandable loss for them both. Losing one's active role as a mother creates painful feelings.

One woman sees this as an opportunity to pursue new challenges and interests, while the other will get "stuck," grieving her losses. The second one's persistently negative thoughts will lead to anxious feelings which can, in turn, trigger depression. Both are experiencing the same event, but their interpretations of the event are notably different.

In life, stress and loss are inevitable. The key is to handle stress in healthy ways in order to stay balanced. Healthful habits build up resistance and help women weather the storms of life. When they don't take the time to refresh themselves during stressful times, women leave themselves vulnerable to exhaustion and a worsening mental outlook.

When the scale is tipped out of balance, when we don't take care of ourselves, we can end up with any number of depressive disorders. We'll look at these next.

Questions for reflection and discussion:

1) What are some specific things you can do to keep yourself healthy and balanced?

2) Are there one or two areas of your life that are out of balance now?

3) If you are currently experiencing depression, can you identify an event or person that "tipped the scales" out of balance?

CHAPTER 6

MAJOR DEPRESSION

Depression comes in many shades of gray. It is not a one-size-fits-all illness, nor is it a respecter of persons. Depression visits the old and the young, the rich and the poor. It is as unique as each individual who is "fearfully and wonderfully made."

We are affected by depression differently because each of us has a unique make-up emotionally, spiritually, physically, and relationally. Some have had difficult pasts—abuse, dysfunctional family upbringing, divorce—that strongly influence today's emotions and thinking processes. Genetics can also play a part in the development of depression.

How does depression make itself apparent in a woman? We've already discussed the difference between adjustment disorders—those things that can cause a low mood for a shorter period of time—and a depressive episode. Depression reveals itself in a number of different ways which we will look at in turn: major depression, dysthymia, seasonal affective disorder (SAD), postpartum depression, and bipolar disorder.

The key symptom of major depression is the inability to function day-to-day. A woman with this type of depression finds it difficult to work, interact socially with others, take care of herself or her home, think positively about herself, or feel spiritually connected to God. Severe depression affects every facet of a woman's life; no area is left untouched.

There are several symptoms doctors look for in making a diagnosis of major depression. At least five of the following seven symptoms must be present. They must last a minimum of two weeks and change how a person normally functions. Symptoms include:

- Depressed mood
- Diminished interest or pleasure in activities
- Significant appetite loss or gain; significant weight loss or gain
- Insomnia or hypersomnia (excessive sleeping)
- Feelings of worthlessness or excessive guilt
- Diminished ability to think or concentrate
- Recurrent thoughts of death or suicide[1]

As you can see, a number of different factors must be met to establish a diagnosis of major depression. In total, these include changes in mood, energy, and feelings of self-worth. For a Christian woman, one of the more painful aspects of major depression is the feeling of abandonment by God.

Cheryl, the nurse whom we met earlier, described her feelings this way: "I remember that as I was becoming depressed I started really feeling distant from God. I wanted to reach out to Him and have Him reach back, but I felt Him slipping away. I just couldn't connect with

God. I still believed that Christ loved me and that He was my Savior, but, as far as a personal relationship, I felt like there was a barrier between us and He was on the other side."

Major depression also impacts a woman's life relationally. This is particularly painful for women because God designed us to be relational beings. The inability to connect with other people causes emotional distress and guilt. I recall starting to withdraw from family and friends. Without the stamina to socialize, I avoided people. I would always consider the energy it would cost me if I chose to meet with someone.

It seems so foolish now, this lack of desire to be with others I loved and cared for, but that was my reality at the time. Withdrawing also left me with a terrible feeling of loneliness as I was emotionally and physically trapped at home with no desire to see anyone or go anywhere.

We will look at available treatments for major depression later in the book, but for now let's turn our attention to a chronic form of depression called *dysthymia*.

Questions for reflection and discussion:

1) How many of these symptoms of depression can you identify with: depressed mood, diminished interest or pleasure in activities, significant appetite gain or loss, insomnia or excessive sleeping, feelings of worthlessness, excessive guilt, reduced ability to think or concentrate, recurrent thoughts of death or suicide?

2) Have you noticed changes in your mood, energy level, or feelings of self-worth?

3) What have you had to give up because of your depression?

4) Do you feel that God is distant or uncaring? What do you think contributes to these feelings of separation from God?

CHAPTER 7

DYSTHYMIA

Major depression, while severe in nature, is relatively short-lived in comparison to *dysthymia*. For a woman to be diagnosed with this type of depression her symptoms must last more than two years without a break for more than two months.[1]

Identified as "chronic" because of its long-term nature, dysthymia is still painful for women who suffer with it. Much like a low-grade fever or infection, dysthymia is considered a low-grade depression that leaves the woman feeling discouraged and inadequate.

Tabor's Medical Dictionary breaks down the word dysthymia into two parts: *dys-*, meaning difficult or painful, and *thymos,* meaning "mind."[2] Therefore, dysthymia means "painful mind," characterizing the negativity and sadness that accompanies this form of depression.

Symptoms are similar to major depression only not as severe or of the same quantity. While dysthymia causes some emotional upset and lower energy levels, it is not all-consuming like major depression. Feelings of hopelessness or worthlessness are not as common with dysthymia, and the person is able to function day-to-day.

One of the more painful aspects of dysthymia, though, occurs when family members and friends begin to see the person's symptoms as part of their personality, considering their behavior "normal." It becomes acceptable to view them as having a low energy level, low self-esteem, and poor concentration much of the time.

Episodes of major depression can also occur from time to time with dysthymia, since stress causes the person to get out of balance physically and emotionally.

The goal of treatment is to lift the chronic low mood so the individual can experience the joy and fullness of life that God intends for them.

Questions for reflection and discussion:

1) How is dysthymia different from major depression?

2) What type of label is frequently attached to someone with dysthymia?

CHAPTER 8

SEASONAL AFFECTIVE DISORDER

Fall is my favorite time of year. We live where the summers are hot and uncomfortable, so autumn's cool breezes provide a reprieve from the heat and humidity. The trees in our neighborhood turn beautiful shades of yellow, orange, and red. So what is wrong with this lovely picture? Seasonal affective disorder. It strikes every fall around the time when daylight savings time ends and shorter days of light begin, bringing with it a season-long depression.

Seasonal affective disorder, also known as SAD, is the only form of depression with a predictable pattern. As the days become shorter, depressive symptoms start to set in: cravings for carbohydrates, weight gain, a lack of energy, being anxious or irritable, having an increased desire for sleep, or withdrawing socially. It's much like a bear preparing to hibernate through the winter!

Many sensitive people become clinically depressed every fall, while symptoms tend to improve in the spring. Researchers believe the amount of sunlight exposure affects the production and use of body chemicals, including serotonin and norepinephrine, the two neurotransmitters most associated with depression.[1]

Low light also increases the amount of a sleep hormone, melatonin, which is released in the brain in response to darkness. This explains the need for more sleep. A diagnosis of SAD is made when symptoms recur at the same time every year, for at least two years in a row, and symptoms resolve with the change of seasons.[2]

Although there is no known cure for SAD, the depression can be lifted through counseling or the use of antidepressant medications during fall and winter. Depressive symptoms can also be relieved by the use of phototherapy: full-spectrum fluorescent lights that mimic the sun's rays. Known as a light box, the individual sits in front of the lamp for 30-60 minutes each morning, effectively replacing the sunlight lost by being indoors in the winter months.

Light boxes can be purchased over the Internet but be sure to choose one that has a minimum of 10,000 Lux, a measure of brightness. The only side effects are agitation or headache caused by too much time in front of the light. Phototherapy can make a difference for many people, turning a dreaded time of year into one that is positive and hopeful.

Questions for reflection and discussion:

1) Why is SAD [seasonal affective disorder] more common in the fall and winter?

2) Have you had experience using a light box? If so, how has it helped?

SAD

Lord, I waited for Your sun today,
        But 'lo it did not shine.
I paused to wonder where it might be.
        Behind the haze, I could not see.

So dim the sky,
        Not far from night.
Where, oh Lord,
        Is Your fair light?

My soul feels like the gray-filled day.
        You seem so very far away.
Dear Lord, will You sustain my mood
        When all I want is sleep and food?

Why do you hide above the clouds,
        Where eagles soar
            And planes are bound,
The place where glory can be found?

Won't you bend Your sweet sun down
        To light the sky, the trees, the ground?
Please take this sadness from my heart,
        Your brilliant light, to me impart.

I want to move into this day
        With confidence that You will stay
            Bright and clear up in the sky;
'O Light of Day, won't you draw nigh?

CHAPTER 9

POSTPARTUM DEPRESSION

There is perhaps no greater joy than bringing a new life into the world. The nine months of pregnancy not only prepare the baby for life outside the womb but also prepare the soon-to-be parents for the changes to come.

I remember fondly the day we brought our first-born home from the hospital. There was an early December snow falling; the world was bright with promise. The hospital nurse carefully buckled our newborn son into the backseat of the car.

As we pulled away from the hospital, an overwhelming sense of responsibility for this little one settled on my shoulders. Would I be a good mother? Would I be able to care for all his needs?

After a few days at home, catching up on my sleep while my mother cared for Matthew, I began to feel more comfortable with my new role. Breastfeeding was going well and Matthew was gaining weight, so I knew that everything would be fine.

Such feelings of responsibility can lead many women to feel weary, teary, and anxious. Are such troubling feelings normal? Findings show that 70-80% of women have the "baby blues" shortly after childbirth. They may find themselves crying for no reason or having doubts about their ability to be a good mother; however, they are still able to care for themselves and their baby. These disturbing feelings can be the result of shifting hormone levels after birth and while breastfeeding, but generally last no more than a few days after delivery.[1]

While a short period of baby blues can be expected, 10% of all mothers will experience more severe symptoms known as postpartum depression. In general, PPD starts 1-3 weeks after delivery and is thought to be the result of low estrogen levels and sleep disruptions.[2]

Symptoms are similar to major depression and include feelings of sadness, doubt, guilt, and helplessness. The mother may lose interest in her baby and not be able to care for the infant or herself. Even more serious, she may have concerns about hurting her baby. When the depression reaches this point, loving family and friends need to step in to help the distraught mother.

A supportive doctor can provide counseling or prescribe an antidepressant medication. An estrogen hormone patch can help restore the balance of hormones gone awry.

With adequate support from family, appropriate medication, and counseling, most mothers experiencing PPD will find relief and can go on to experience the joys of nurturing their newborn.

Questions for reflection and discussion:

1) What is the difference between the baby blues and postpartum depression?

2) If you are a mother, did you experience any of the symptoms described in this chapter following the birth of your baby? Explain.

CHAPTER 10

BIPOLAR DISORDER

Among my fondest childhood memories were times spent at my grandparents' cabin in Nebraska. Perched above a sandpit lake, the beaches surrounding their cabin provided endless entertainment for my siblings and me. On one side of the cabin was a teeter-totter my grandfather made for his grandchildren. We traveled up and down on that teeter-totter until we were worn out. It was exhilarating to reach the top, but painful to hit bottom. And if my sibling happened to jump off unexpectedly, the quick thud to the ground jarred my whole body.

Bipolar disorder is much like that teeter-totter: exhilarating when a person is "up;" discouraged and defeated when they're "down." Previously known as manic-depressive disorder, the term *bipolar* means living in one of two extremes or "poles": manic or depressed. While there may be stretches of time with normal moods, it is more common to experience one extreme or the other.

Symptoms of major depression are common with bipolar disorder. The depressive episodes generally outnumber the manias and last for longer periods of time.

Terri, the graduate student whom we met earlier, learned to be aware of the signs that depression was imminent. "When my sleep schedule started getting off track and I found myself becoming more controlling and obsessive about things, I knew that depression was right around the corner. It's a pretty slippery slope once it starts, but my family has also learned to recognize the signs and be more supportive during those times."

During the manic phase of bipolar disorder the mind is filled with grand ideas and the energy to go with them. Projects are started but never finished; the person becomes more talkative than usual and is easily distracted. They need less sleep and often go several days without sleeping. Impulsive behavior is also common, leading to spending sprees with credit cards or acting out sexually.[1]

There is also a milder form of mania called hypomania. Characterized by milder symptoms than seen in a true mania, the individual experiences greater energy, creativity, and productivity. Symptoms don't cause as much disruption to mood or the ability to function normally. For those whose bipolar disorder is primarily depressive in nature, the upbeat feelings of hypomania can be a welcome relief. However, following a manic or hypomanic episode, the person can crash again into the depths of depression.[2]

It's good to be aware that relief might be short-lived when dealing with bipolar disorder and not be taken by surprise when the depression returns. People need to be vigilant to keep their thought life, activities, and relationships balanced to help prevent the slide into the depressive side of bipolar.

Researchers have found a strong biological or genetic predisposition to bipolar disorder, meaning that it tends to run in families. When Cheryl, the nurse who we met in Chapter 4, was diagnosed with bipolar disorder, she recalled her mother's struggles with long periods of depression interspersed with times of great energy and enthusiasm. This behavior seemed normal to the rest of the family.

Cheryl now takes a medication known as a mood stabilizer to help prevent roller coaster emotions. The medication helps prevent the extreme highs and lows of being bipolar, and keeps her mood stable, which is the goal of treatment.

Questions for reflection and discussion:

1) Do you ever experience "roller-coaster" moods? If so, can you identify specific triggers for a high or low?

2) Can you think of anyone in your family (a parent, grandparent, sibling, aunt, uncle, cousin) who currently has (or had in the past) a mood disorder? You may have to do some searching of your family tree or talk to relatives to find answers.

CHAPTER 11

THE PERSONALITY PUZZLE

From birth, each of my children were unique in their temperaments. Matthew was a curious baby and a child of detail and creativity. Kelly was an easy baby and a delightful girl—gentle and kind, often listening but seldom talking unless something important needed to be said. Kevin was our easy-going baby and our entertaining, laid-back child—engaging people from the time he learned to talk.

What my husband and I saw in their childhood temperaments grew with them into adulthood. Nothing in their growing-up experience could change their inborn traits. Matthew is now a gifted writer, majoring in philosophy at college. Kelly is a peacemaker, a servant on the mission field. Kevin is a young man of adventure, trying many things and enjoying everybody along the way.

I believe God shaped a unique temperament for each of us, one that would accomplish His purposes. God's Word tells us that we are fearfully and wonderfully made, woven together in our mother's womb, and that He is intimately acquainted with all our ways (Ps. 139:3,14,15). This includes our temperament.

As a child grows, temperament unfolds like the petals of a flower to reveal personality, the part of us that communicates to others who we are inside. Personality is also shaped by the environment in which we are raised and the influence of our family. Birth order is also thought to have a strong influence on a child's personality.

Personality types were first identified by Hippocrates, a Greek physician and philosopher, nearly 2,500 years ago. It was his determination that there were four basic temperaments, each named for a fluid in the body: Sanguine (blood), Choleric (yellow bile), Melancholy (black bile) and Phlegmatic (phlegm).[1] More recent classifications of temperament and personality include extrovert/introvert and the sixteen-fold Myers-Briggs Type Indicator (MBTI).

It needs to be understood that people of all temperaments can experience depression, particularly if influenced by one's genes or environment. However, there is one temperament that is more susceptible to depression than the others: the Melancholy. Several unique characteristics of the Melancholy make this temperament more vulnerable to experiencing depressive episodes.

Let's begin by looking at a female Melancholy's strengths, because she has so much to offer those around her. These women are complex, characterized by deep thinking and introspection. They are sensitive to and aware of their thoughts and feelings. Melancholies can be the most creative of all the temperaments, and many become artists, musicians, and writers. They are sensitive to the world around them and find inspiration and spiritual refreshment in nature.

On the practical side, Melancholies are the women

who pay attention to details and love to plan and organize in the home and workplace. The way they think is methodical and orderly, and they set high standards for both themselves and others. My husband and I learned the hard way that it's best to ask a Melancholy to help paint your house rather than a more talkative, fun-loving Sanguine. Attention to detail is definitely not the Sanguine's forte!

Let's turn a corner and examine a few of the Melancholy's weaknesses and how they leave a woman vulnerable to depression. Melancholies come into the world with a serious nature. Their ability to think deeply enables them to look at the positive and negative side of every situation and decision. My husband is the eternal optimist and sees me—a Melancholy—as the least positive thinker in the family. Whenever he lovingly criticizes my attitude, I just tell him I'm being realistic!

Because of their serious nature, Melancholies are perfectionists and place extreme pressure on themselves to be orderly and organized. If circumstances frustrate their ability to maintain this level, they quickly become discouraged. How easy it is then to view themselves as a failure, berating themselves for not living up to their unrealistically high standards. They also internalize stressful situations and can become easily overwhelmed.

Spiritually, the Melancholy harbors a deep-seated fear that she is letting God down by her performance. Her self-critical attitude causes her to feel that she never quite measures up to God's perceived demands. As Betty Southard and Marita Littauer point out in their book *Come As You Are*, "High personal expectations and standards keep the Perfect Melancholy from experiencing the love and acceptance that God offers to her."[2] Sadly, she may feel like a failure and give up working on her relationship with God altogether.

How easily the Melancholy can get out-of-balance! Her negative thinking can lead to depression and anxiety disorders. More than anything, Melancholies need to accept themselves as God created them and not be so hard on themselves. When negative thoughts threaten to weigh them down, the best thing to do is follow Jesus' teaching to "take every thought captive to the obedience of Christ" (2 Cor. 10:5). Replacing those negative thoughts with Truth will lead Melancholy women to a more balanced viewpoint of themselves and God. Celebrating one's strengths and acknowledging weaknesses helps these women become more resilient in their emotional life and lessen the chances of depression.

Questions for reflection and discussion:

1) If you have children, have you been able to identify characteristics of their temperament? How are these characteristics expressed in each one's personality?

2) What can you, as a parent, do to nurture the positive qualities you see in your child?

3) Which of the Melancholy's strengths do you most admire? Which weaknesses do you see in your own life?

4) All of us can, at times, be hard on ourselves and feel that we fall short. How could you push aside those negative thoughts to see yourself as God loves and accepts you?

CHAPTER 12

WOMEN AND DEPRESSION

Did you know that twice as many women as men suffer from depression in this country? What accounts for this gap between the genders? Some researchers believe that more women report being depressed than do their male counterparts or that men mask their depression with drugs, alcohol, or workaholism. Others say it is the unique emotional make-up of women that leaves them more vulnerable to depressive illnesses. Still others claim that women's multiple roles and responsibilities are the culprit. Let's look at how the sexes differ in terms of depression.

In the spiritual realm, women are a likely target for the Enemy's attack. Consider that the Enemy first approached Eve in the Garden rather than her husband. Was it her tender, compassionate soul that caused her to incline her ear to the serpent? Was she captivated by his beauty? After all, we women have an eye for all things beautiful.

We are by no means the "weaker sex," as some have said. Each of us is powerful in the strength God gives us to manage our many responsibilities. He uses the power of our emotions to energize us to care for and love the people around us. At those times when we feel weak and ineffective, we need only to remind ourselves of Paul's words in 2 Corinthians 12:9-10, "My grace is sufficient for you, for my power is made perfect in weakness… For when I am weak, then I am strong" (NIV).

While God designed both genders to be relational beings, He gave women the unique ability to focus specifically on relationships. Over the years, as I helped in the preschool Sunday school class at church, I began to see differences in the way boys and girls interacted with those around them.

Little girls would play cooperatively with one another while the boys were more comfortable playing alone or side-by-side. Girls were more likely to make eye contact and talk to the other girls in the group while motor noises were much more common with the boys. The girls were also more likely to engage their teachers or sit on adult laps for Bible story time, whereas the boys preferred to stretch out on the floor, hands propped under little chins.

As my own children were growing up, I saw in their friendships similar qualities. Matthew and Kevin were most comfortable playing alone with cars and building blocks, while Kelly wasn't happy unless her brothers or friends were there to play with her. In high school, I noticed that the girls moved in larger circles than the boys who were usually seen with one or two friends at the most. As adults, women are more likely to have many friendships while men generally have only one or two close relationships, and one of those is likely to be with his wife!

Since relationships and emotional support are so

vital to women, it makes sense that when these are interrupted, problems arise. Difficulties and conflict in relationships can lead to feelings of discouragement. So can emotional isolation resulting from a move or major change. In fact, women are so sensitive to relationships that when a friend hasn't called in awhile, we think she no longer likes us. A man would think nothing of it or at least not take it personally.

Women also have unique stressors that can trigger depression, whereas the same stresses may not have the same impact on men. Women lack "self time" where they can relax and rejuvenate, often because they are so focused on caring for the needs of others. Many of the parenting responsibilities fall on women's shoulders in addition to having to care for the house and meals. Working outside the home can add to these stresses. It's no wonder more women don't crash trying to juggle it all!

Hormones affect women differently than men and may account for a greater prevalence of depression. We deal with PMS, periods, pregnancies, postpartum upsets, perimenopause and, finally, menopause. Men have one primary hormone, testosterone, which accounts for their manly characteristics. Male hormones don't roller coaster each month as ours do.

Cultural expectations also impact more women than men. How many men do you know that stress over how their bodies look? How their clothes fit? How they compare to the men around them? Sounds almost silly, doesn't it?

But we do compare ourselves to the women in our relationships and those we see on TV and in magazines.

Weight issues can be particularly problematic as they affect our sense of self-worth. If we don't measure up to societal expectations, we feel like a failure. Enough feelings of failure and we can slip into depression.

Women are also more emotional than men. Just as a camera lens brings a scene into focus, so we see all of life through an emotional lens that colors everything around us. Men are just the opposite. They tend to focus their lens on practical matters and objects. At times they can have difficulty experiencing and understanding their emotions.

As women, the problem with seeing life through an emotional filter is that we can become overly sensitive to everything inside and around us. How we manage this flow of feelings and our perceptions of people and events will have a major impact on our mental state.

Spiritual attacks, relationships, stress, hormones, cultural expectations, and emotions—one or any combination can contribute to the higher incidence of depression in women than in men. Not a weaker sex, not a "less than," God created women with just the right qualities our world needs. Celebrate your strengths! He made you the way you are for a reason, and He can use your weaknesses for good if you let Him. Be encouraged that not every weakness leads to depression.

Questions for reflection and discussion:

1) In your own opinion, why do you think it's more common for women to be depressed than men?

2) What are some of the drawbacks of being focused on relationships, as women tend to be?

3) What are some of the blessings of being relationally focused?

CHAPTER 13

THE WHYS OF DEPRESSION

Sitting across the desk from the doctor, you hear the word "cancer." It rings so loudly in your ear that every sentence to follow is drowned out by the noise. You think, *Why me?*

A friend and her family are in a bad car accident. The other car ran a red light. The husband is in a coma with serious head injuries. *Why them?*

A young soldier, fresh out of basic training, a few months out of high school, is called up to serve his country. The fighting is intense where he's going. *Why now?*

Life is full of *why* questions. That's where faith steps in and fills the gap, faith that is hard won by practice and perseverance. Faith that God will use all things for our good as we trust in Him, especially when we don't understand.

Depression is also filled with *why* questions: *Why do I feel so bad? Why don't I feel like doing anything? Why do I feel so ashamed?* This chapter is written to offer you hope when the *why* questions are raised.

The first question is this: *Why do I feel so bad?* Depressed women feel bad for a number of reasons. One primary cause, as we looked at earlier, is that several of the brain chemicals—neurotransmitters—that control mood are either in short supply or not working properly. As a result, you may begin to experience symptoms of fatigue, apathy, change in appetite, and depressed mood. Medications are the best source of healing because they return these chemicals to their proper balance in the brain.

Other changes in the body can fuel feeling bad—conditions like low thyroid function, migraine headaches, chronic pain, and hormone changes.

Feeling bad is also caused by our inability to do the things that would help us feel better. Other people, wanting to be helpful, offer their sincere suggestions. A good friend encouraged me to exercise, because it always made *her* feel better. A well-intentioned suggestion, it was hurtful nonetheless since I knew I didn't have the energy to walk on my treadmill. I felt guilty that I couldn't exercise or at least follow my friend's advice.

Other friends suggested vitamins or health foods to strengthen my body. Since I didn't have the energy to cook healthy meals, my husband and I fell back on less-healthy fast food. I felt bad that I wasn't able to fix nutritious food for the two of us.

Another *why* question has to do with our vitality: *Why do I have so little energy?* Depression has a way of slowing you down mentally and physically. At times, you may feel completely shut down. When you feel good, you don't even consider the energy it takes to perform daily functions—you just do them. When you feel bad, it takes great effort to climb out of bed, get off the couch, or take on the day.

I spent my days doing number puzzles. It took little energy yet gave me a feeling of accomplishment. It is discouraging to live in a world that has shrunk in size because you don't have the energy to get out and enjoy it.

Why don't I feel like doing anything? This question closely ties in with a lack of energy. The problem here is that you may lack the motivation to do things you once enjoyed. When I was depressed, I gave up hobbies and interests that once brought me pleasure. I had little motivation for any of them.

I experienced a general sense of apathy. I didn't seem to care for anyone or anything. I lacked the desire to get out and see people, to share meals and activities together. I felt particularly sad for my husband as I lost all interest in intimacy. I didn't have the energy or desire for closeness. I just wanted to be left alone.

Why can't I concentrate? This becomes particularly difficult if you work outside the home. An employee is expected to be engaged in her work, making decisions and performing tasks with deadlines and quotas in mind. If you can't concentrate enough to read, write, or do your job proficiently, it can cause serious problems. You may even feel that your job is in jeopardy, as Debbie did, especially if you take time off because of the depressive symptoms. If you work and serve at home, concentration to clean, cook, or care for children can be in short supply.

Cheryl took some time off from her hospital job, a career that requires detailed concentration. Though she missed her co-workers, she knew it was important to step aside for a time to keep her patients safe.

Tracy, 33, and an administrative assistant, was able

to cut back on her hours at the insurance company where she worked. It helped her keep stress to a minimum so she could concentrate when she was at the office.

Denise, a mother of three, took her children to a Mother's Day Out program at her church so she could relax and catch up on things at home.

Why do I feel so lonely? Depression is isolating. Due to a lack of energy and motivation, depressed women seldom get out to see people or socialize. You may find it difficult to engage with family members or do pleasurable activities with them. It's hard to put into words how you feel, and even when you are able to share your feelings, others don't seem to understand. I found this to be a very difficult aspect of depression and it fed my loneliness.

Depressed women tend to have higher expectations of receiving support and understanding from people in their church. When they don't receive it, they become discouraged and bitter, reinforcing their separation from others. Enough discouraging comments from church members and it's no wonder these women withdraw into loneliness.

Why do I feel ashamed? There is perhaps no more damaging emotion to the human psyche than shame. It destroys one's sense of self-worth and hope for the future. Feelings of guilt can be dealt with by asking for God's forgiveness and cleansing, but shame does little to motivate women toward spiritual health.

Many aspects of depression fuel feelings of shame. When you can't function normally it makes you feel lazy. Nike didn't have it completely right when they said "Just Do It" in their ad campaign from years ago. Those who are depressed would "just do it" if only they could.

Others say to "just get over it." Such comments are discouraging and lead to guilt over not being able to function normally. Shame is fueled by the stigma toward mental illnesses in our society and the church. What is misunderstood is not fully accepted by either one.

Feeling bad, lacking in energy, unmotivated, unable to concentrate, feeling lonely and ashamed—all are part of the *whys* of depression. More than trying to provide answers to these questions, my intention has been to come alongside and say that it's ok to feel the way you do.

You are not abnormal. You have permission to feel this way because your thoughts and feelings are normal for someone who is experiencing depression. Please know that you are not alone in your painful feelings. Everyone with depression experiences them to one extent or another.

You are who you are by God's grace, and He is with you in your depression. He understands your loneliness—He is beside you when others aren't. He understands your lack of energy and motivation–He loves you not for what you can or can't do but because of who you are, His precious child. He understands your shame— He knows it is from the Enemy, trying to separate you from God and other people. Keep focusing on the Truth even in the midst of your doubt and discouragement. He desires your healing and will never abandon you to the painful *whys* of depression.

Questions for reflection and discussion:

1) What role does faith play when we are consumed with the "why" questions related to our depression?

2) How are you limited by a lack of energy or motivation to carry out your daily responsibilities?

3) Does your depression cause you to feel isolated or lonely? If so, why?

4) Have you ever been told to "just get over it" by well-meaning friends or family members? How did that make you feel?

5) Do you believe God understands what you are going through and that He is willing and able to help you walk through the depression?

6) Do you have a favorite Bible promise that you cling to? You may want to refer to the list of encouraging scriptures that are listed at the end of the book.

CHAPTER 14

HOPE FOR HEALING

Where do I go to get help? If you are concerned that you may be depressed—that is, your symptoms have lasted two weeks or more—make a phone call to your family physician or internist. They are always your greatest resource when it comes to primary medical care. Blood tests and a complete physical can rule out any medical issues that may be causing the depression, such as a sluggish thyroid or chronic pain.

If needed, your doctor can prescribe medication (an antidepressant) to address your symptoms. More difficult cases can be referred to a psychiatrist, a doctor who specializes in the care of those with mental illnesses. They are more familiar with drugs used to treat depression and mood disorders and have a better understanding of how combinations of medications work together to bring healing.

How is depression treated? For those with mild to moderate depression, psychotherapy may offer the best treatment. A therapist will educate you on depression, provide a safe place where you can share your feelings, and help you deal with any losses that may have triggered your depression.

Therapists include psychologists, licensed mental health professionals, and clinical social workers. You will find them in private practices or in mental health clinics. Ask your family physician for a referral, or ask for a recommendation from a pastor or friend. A Christian counselor may be the most helpful as he or she can address the spiritual side of depression in addition to the physical, emotional, and mental aspects.

Psychotherapy includes talk therapy and relaxation exercises for those who find that anxiety is also an issue. During talk therapy you will explore any painful thoughts or moods you are experiencing. A specific type of therapy, cognitive behavioral therapy, helps individuals identify false or negative thoughts and replace them with truthful, positive ones. The Bible offers its own prescription in Romans 12:2 where we are told to "be transformed by the renewing of your mind."

Another type of therapy, interpersonal therapy, focuses on the depressed person's relationships, helping them learn more positive ways of interacting and communicating with others.

For severe depression or bipolar disorder, your doctor may prescribe an antidepressant or mood stabilizer. Once the brain chemicals affecting mood become unbalanced, medication will almost certainly be needed to restore the neurotransmitters to a normal level.

If your pancreas does not function well, causing you to have diabetes, you would not deny yourself the medication needed to help your body work properly. So why would you reject medication that will restore your mood and energy level? It's important to point out here that psychologists and therapists are not able to prescribe medications. You will need to see your family physician or a psychiatrist to obtain an antidepressant.

Is medication always necessary? Pride issues often stand in the way when a doctor recommends treatment with medication. Since we live in a society that values independence, you may tell yourself, *I can beat this depression on my own. I don't need anyone's help.* Perhaps because you think "it's all in my head," you feel that depressive symptoms can be overcome merely by willpower.

Christians can put unnecessary pressure on themselves to seek healing for depression through prayer and Bible reading *to the exclusion of medical treatment or counseling.* I believe it's vital to address both the spiritual and the physical to bring about complete healing. Medication serves to bring the body back into balance, while counseling and spiritual practices help heal the issues that have triggered the depression. Don't let pride or the opinion of others less knowledgeable about depression keep you from getting the necessary treatment.

What if I feel worse instead of better on an antidepressant? Side effects are common with all drugs, including those taken for depression. Common side effects of antidepressants include dizziness, tiredness, nausea, headache, increased sweating, diarrhea or constipation, sexual difficulties, and trouble sleeping. They can be minimized by starting at a low dosage and working up gradually to a level that provides relief from symptoms.

I recall those first frustrating weeks on an antidepressant. I wanted to feel better right away, like taking an aspirin for a headache. Instead, I felt discouraged.

I realize now that my frustration resulted from a lack of patience, a quality that is so important in those first few weeks of treatment. It took three to four weeks for my energy level to pick up, followed by a very gradual improvement in my mood.

You may find that your first antidepressant brings maximum relief, or you may be one of those who need to "trial" a few medications until the right one is found. Sometimes a second or third medication is added to improve the effectiveness of the first. When I was no longer getting better, my doctor recommended a second medication which helped considerably. Over time I've had my dosage fine-tuned so that I can continue to enjoy a stable mood and energy level.

Your doctor will also determine how long you will need to continue taking the antidepressant. Four to six months is a general guideline, although the length of time can be indefinite if you've had several depressive episodes.

If you continue to feel poorly while on medication, don't assume this will be as good as it gets. No one should settle for being "just ok" if you can feel your best on a higher dose or a different medication. Overall, it takes a commitment to work with your doctor and have regular follow-up visits so he or she can determine if your medication is working effectively.

How do I involve my family in the healing process? Explaining your condition to family and friends is one of the more difficult aspects of depression. You may wonder, *Will they think I'm crazy?* Such thoughts arise from the stigma that is still present in our society toward mental illnesses. It's difficult to accept something you don't fully understand, so it's your job to help your loved ones understand your mental condition.

Explain to your family and friends that depression is not something you can beat on your own. You will need a support team of loved ones, doctors, therapists, and caring friends. Enlist their help as members of your support team. Help them understand that there will be times when you will turn down invitations to take part in social gatherings.

It's important that they know your depression is not a personal rejection of their love when you don't want to see or talk to them. They need to know that the depression cannot be overcome by your own willpower. Explain the role of medication or psychotherapy in your recovery plan and why one or both are needed for you to experience relief from your symptoms.

No one need suffer in silence and isolation when help is available. As we've learned, medications, primary-care physicians, psychiatrists, counselors, and family all serve to support the healing process. As you take advantage of these various avenues of help, your sense of hope that healing is possible is rekindled. And in the words of the Apostle Paul, "hope does not disappoint" (Rom. 5:5).

Questions for reflection and discussion:

1) Where have you sought help for your depression?

2) Is there a particular treatment that has improved your depressive symptoms?

3) What is your personal belief regarding whether a Christian should take medication for depression? Do you believe medication alone can cure depression?

4) If you've had more than one episode of depression, and your doctor has recommended that you stay on medication for an unspecified length of time, how do you feel about this?

CHAPTER 15

WHERE IS GOD WHEN I NEED HIM?

Feelings of abandonment by God are common among women who struggle with depression. The nature of the disease causes you to be self-focused, turning your thoughts inward on yourself. And when you are entirely focused on yourself, it can be difficult to relate to others and to the Lord. It's hard to sense God's love and presence when you feel ashamed and unworthy in your relationship with Him.

Not only are depressed women self-focused, they also find it difficult to connect with God in prayer or through his Word. Lack of concentration may make it nearly impossible for you to understand what the Bible says. You may read a few sentences over and over, yet fail to comprehend their meaning.

In prayer, you may find it particularly challenging to stay focused on a conversation with God, both through speaking and listening. Your own internal thoughts can be a distraction, as well as things going on around you.

I understand that the spiritual impact of depression is painful, particularly if you've had a close walk with God up until now. To lessen the anxiety and shame about your relationship with the Lord, let's hear from some women who have been where you are. What you are experiencing is not uncommon for those who are depressed.

Terri, the graduate student, shares, "At times when I need God the most, when I'm down and out and in complete despair, I can't talk to Him at all. It's like there's a glass wall that separates me from him. Everything I try to direct toward God just bounces back to me."

Cheryl also sensed a barrier between her and God that seemed impossible to overcome. "Thinking of Jesus being far away was very distressing to me. I was lost and couldn't find Him. By faith I never doubted Jesus was there, but I wasn't able to commune with Him or even sense He was there."

Spiritual attack was addressed by several women who struggled with feeling disconnected from God. Sandi, a mother of twin girls, put it most succinctly when she said, "I think there was some spiritual wrestling going on for me, feeling like 'Where's God?'. I wonder if the Enemy senses when you're starting to feel better and wants to keep you down as long as possible. He plants negative thoughts that God has abandoned me. So not only am I fighting depression, there is spiritual warfare on top of that. You compound that by feeling you can't talk to God and it's like being kicked when you're down."

And finally, Kathleen, 54, touched on the shame she felt in her relationship with God. "I remember wondering how I'd gotten into such bad shape. I did blame myself much more. I was upset with myself. I felt there must be something I was not doing in my relationship with God."

Each of these women expressed a feeling of separation from God and the guilt that accompanies such thoughts. In the next chapter we will look at how one's faith is impacted by depression.

Questions for reflection and discussion:

1) What words would you use to describe your relationship with God since your depression?

2) In what ways have you tried to connect with God during your depression? Have these experiences been positive, negative, or neutral?

3) What can you do to find relief from your feelings of shame or guilt as you think about your spiritual struggles?

CHAPTER 16

FAITH ISSUES

The inspired writers of the New Testament offer a definition of faith in Hebrews 11:1: "Now faith is the assurance of things hoped for, the conviction of things not seen." Faith implies a steady confidence in God and the promises of his Word. Part of this definition is the confident "assurance of things hoped for"—hope for the future and hope for this life on earth. But what should you do, how are you to think, when faith falters and hope disappears?

The experience of depression is closely intertwined with our spiritual life; that is, we cannot experience depression without it affecting our faith in God. Depression shakes us to the very core of who we are as a person—that place where our sense of self and life purpose reside.

One physician put it this way: "Depression is, in many ways, the worst of diseases because it hits patients where they are the most vulnerable, by robbing them of their sense of self-worth and calling into question their very reason for being."[1]

The deepest pain I experienced during my depression was this: *If I can't be the person God created me to be, if I can't use my strengths and gifts to serve others as God intends, then where is my hope for living?* The thought caused me to question my value in the eyes of God. It stole my hope as surely as the night steals the last glimmer of day.

Perhaps you have wrestled with this issue of hope in your own depression. As much as you long to grab hold of hope and God's love for you, they are painfully absent when you are in the depths of depression. There seems to be little to cling to spiritually when depression has its grip on your heart.

Author Paul David Tripp speaks of this pain when he says, "Being a believer does not exempt you from moments of significant darkness….There will be moments when it seems like you are utterly alone and that no one could possibly understand what you are going through."[2]

Yet in the midst of darkness and hopelessness, there is good news—the Truth—that your feelings do not define who God is or His plans for your life. How easily we can be deceived by our own perceptions of truth, interpreting what we feel and believe in the moment to be true.

We are told in Scripture that "hope does not disappoint, because the love of God has been poured out within our hearts through the Holy Spirit who was given to us" (Rom. 5:5). How can you remain disappointed when the truth is that God's gracious love has been poured out on you? How can you stay discouraged when the Holy Spirit walks beside you in your pain?

How is a quadriplegic like Joni Eareckson Tada any less valuable in God's eyes now than when she wasn't bound to a wheelchair? Or consider the life of a person with Down's syndrome or cerebral palsy. They have no less value because of their mental and physical condition. Then how are you any less valuable because you suffer from depression?

Let's look together at a powerful verse of Scripture that addresses this issue of hope as you see yourself from God's perspective:

> "'For I know the plans that I have for you,' declares the Lord, 'plans for welfare and not for calamity, to give you a future and a hope.
>
> 'Then you will call upon Me and come and pray to Me and I will listen to you. And you will seek Me and find Me, when you search for Me with all your heart. And I will be found by you,' declares the Lord" (Jer. 29:11-14).

Several things stand out to me in this verse that we can apply to our lives. First, God has a good and perfect plan for you. His plans are not for calamity (affliction, distress or ruin). He is looking to bless you instead. Depression is not a curse He inflicts on you.

Secondly, God promises to listen to you as you pray to Him in *the way you are able to at the time*. He understands your inabilities and weaknesses. He takes these things into consideration when looking upon you with His loving eyes. He has given you the Holy Spirit, your Helper, to intercede for you in prayer with "groanings too deep for words" (Rom. 8:26).

Third, God promises that you will find Him. What an awesome promise from our awesome God! When you feel that God is distant and uncaring, the truth is that He longs to draw close to you. He is not in the business of playing hard-to-get. Emotions and clouded vision result in feelings of separation in your relationship with Him.

Choose to believe *in faith* that God is near you and willing to listen and provide comfort. *In faith*, give God permission to tear down the invisible wall that makes you feel He is distant and unreachable. I'm not implying that your feelings of abandonment aren't real. Feelings just are; they are neither right nor wrong but are integral to who you are as a human being created in God's image. Accept your feelings as they are, but don't rely on them as Truth.

God longs for you to invite Him to support you through your journey with depression. He longs to speak to you through His Word—whether through reading or listening—so you will gain a greater understanding of His unconditional love for you. God's Word is a love letter written directly to you so that your faith, hope, and love might be rooted in Him.

Believe and act upon what you know of God. He will not disappoint.

Questions for reflection and discussion:

1) Why do you think it's difficult for women to find hope in the midst of their depression? What is the "good news" the author presents?

2) Do you agree with the physician who was quoted as saying, "Depression is in many ways the worst of diseases because it hits patients where they are the most vulnerable, by robbing them of their sense of self-worth, and calling into question their very reason for being"?

3) Do you believe God loves you unconditionally when you are depressed? What makes it hard for you to accept this truth?

CHAPTER 17

DEPRESSION AND THE CHURCH

Two years prior to my clinical depression, a significant event happened in my life. I was diagnosed with a brain tumor. I had been experiencing severe migraine headaches behind my left eye, along with fatigue. What my physician diagnosed as an on-going sinus infection turned out to be a tumor which became evident on an MRI scan.

Shortly after the diagnosis, I was scheduled for surgery to remove the tumor near the back of my head. The neurosurgeon pointed out the risks of surgery: seizures, temporary blindness in the right eye, and loss of mobility on one side of my body. My family prayed for the grace to be prepared for anything God allowed.

The surgery went well, without any complications. To our relief, pathology tests showed the tumor was not cancerous. Expecting that surgery would resolve the headaches, I was surprised when the fatigue and headaches lasted another nine long months.

My mother and husband were a tremendous support as I recuperated from surgery. They cooked meals, did the laundry, and were there for me throughout my recovery. My church family was supportive as well. They sent cards and brought meals to the house. When I attended church for Easter services just two weeks after the surgery, the women gathered around me, delighted to hear that their prayers were answered and that the tumor was benign.

I share this story of victory over physical illness to point out the contrast to my mental illness. Many in the church knew of the stresses we were experiencing prior to the depression. We'd been members of our evangelical church for eighteen years. I had taught several women's Bible studies, and we were in a couples' small group led by my husband. We were well-known and well-loved by our church family.

However, when I began sliding into the pit of depression, I suddenly found myself alone. Church friends did not call. One or two cards came in the mail. No meals were brought to the house even though cooking was one of the hardest tasks for me to accomplish. A couple in our small group called once and another stopped by briefly to let me know I needed to get over this quickly and not feel sorry for myself. In many ways the rejection by my church family hurt as much as the depression.

Why the different responses? One illness was physical, the other, psychological and emotional. Dr. George Nichols sheds light on this contrast: "Many people still think of depression not as a treatable sickness but as a personal weakness, a lack of willpower, a failure of one's religious faith or a shameful failure of family upbringing."[1]

Many well-meaning people live in denial that there is pain and suffering in the world. They try to avoid it, even reaching a point of numbness due to the continual exposure to suffering on TV, in newspapers, and the movies. This carries over to a lack of compassion and understanding toward those experiencing the suffering of depression.

This bias against the suffering person contributes to their feelings of isolation. Such negative attitudes arise from stigmas, defined as "something that detracts from the character or reputation of a person, group, etc. A mark of disgrace or reproach."[2]

Stigmas arise in our culture and are reflected in the church. For decades there has been a stigma associated with mental illness, primarily from the days of sanitariums for the insane and before there were medications to adequately treat mental disorders. How can we eradicate these stigmas in our churches? I believe it must be through education on the nature of depression and other mental illnesses.

Let's look at two paths of thought on how churches can overcome these stigmas. Quoting from David Biebel and Harold Koenig's insightful book, *New Light On Depression,* "It is high time that the stigma attached by many in the church to their brothers and sisters with depression be exchanged for the attitude the Lord had toward first century lepers, which was to reach out and touch them in loving-kindness when no one else would even go near them."[3]

A second thought, taken from the Life Recovery Bible, shares a similar attitude. "A church should be a hospital for hurting souls, a place where old wounds can be healed and lives can be rebuilt. We all need a healthy church family to help us in the long-term process of recovery."

Lack of understanding among church members causes them to withdraw from those experiencing depression. Many will compare your experience with their own "blue days" when they have a low mood or are feeling discouraged. Just as they can break out of the blues fairly quickly, often by willpower, they expect you to do the same. Well-meaning church members usually offer a spiritual answer such as to pray or read your Bible more.

A similar situation is present when a fellow church member faces a death in the family. We may be at a loss for words to bring comfort to the bereaved person but we do so because we understand their need. With depression (a "death" of normalcy) church members say nothing because they either don't know what to say or fear saying the wrong thing. This creates a situation of isolation for the depressed person.

Let's look at some of the positive things members of a church can do to express love and comfort to depressed women in their congregations. Of first importance is not to ignore her. We wouldn't abandon a grief-stricken member in her time of need and neither should we disregard a woman who is struggling with a depression she did not choose.

The best thing you can do is come alongside her, asking how she is doing and what help is needed. Visit her at home with a meal in hand and take time to listen. Sit beside her and offer to read the Bible. Choose some of David's psalms of hope amidst his discouragement. Read about Job, Jonah, and Jeremiah, with their feelings of abandonment. If you have the Bible on CD or your iPod, share it with her. Listening may be easier than reading at this point in her depression.

Encourage her to get out and do something with you so she doesn't feel socially isolated. Attend a theater performance or a movie. Indulge in a manicure or pedicure; maybe even a new hairstyle. Perhaps what is needed most is a walk around the block or to a nearby park. Getting out in the sunshine can be healing for someone with depression.

When the members of Christ's church step out in faith to minister to those with depressive illnesses, walls of division are torn down. Stigmas are erased, replaced with compassion and understanding. When church leaders begin to accept those with mental illnesses and educate their congregations from the pulpit, depression can be seen for what it is—faulty brain chemistry, not spiritual weakness.

What a blessing it would be if our churches formed depression support groups, giving women a safe place to share their feelings and receive encouragement. I believe the Church can and will rise to the challenge and bring depression out of the closet of shame and into the arms of acceptance.

Questions for reflection and discussion:

1) What were some of the differences in the church's response to the author's physical illness versus her depression?

2) Have you experienced isolation or rejection from your church family? Describe how you feel about it.

3) What can members of your church do to help you in practical ways? How can they minister to you spiritually?

4) If you could be involved in a depression support group for women, how do you think this would help your recovery?

CHAPTER 18

THE ROAD TO RECOVERY

When you think in terms of recovery from depression, you may be tempted to consider only one aspect of healing—your mood. But recovery involves much more than this. Since depression is a whole-person disorder, it follows that healing of the whole person is necessary. This includes physically, mentally, emotionally, relationally, and spiritually. We will look at each of these in turn, exploring different strategies for healing.

We've already spent quite a bit of time focusing on physical recovery. We've looked at the role of medications in restoring brain chemistry to normal. Antidepressants can help you sleep better at night, improve your mood, and restore your energy level. They give you enough vitality so you can begin to work on any issues that may have contributed to the depression. Two other aspects of physical recovery—healthy eating and exercise—will go a long way toward your recovery process as well.

Mental and emotional recovery involves eliminating negative thinking patterns and learning to bring your emotions into balance. A counselor or psychotherapist can assist you in these areas. They will listen to your concerns and help you identify thoughts that may be sabotaging your efforts to heal from the depression. They will help you evaluate those thoughts and call them into question: *Is this really true or just a negative perception?* Whenever I struggle with my own thought life, I am reminded of Philippians 4:8 where Paul says to "fix your thoughts on what is true and honorable and right" (NLT).

A counselor or psychotherapist can also teach you how to handle difficult emotions such as anger, resentment, and hopelessness. Emotions can be powerful, affecting our thought life, motivations, and actions. Try to avoid making decisions based on your feelings. The key is to find balance—to validate your feelings, not deny them, yet not allow them free reign over your mind. We need to take responsibility for our feelings in order to foster healthy relationships and positive mental health.

Be good to yourself. Rediscover those things that in the past brought you pleasure. Maybe you enjoyed creative pursuits such as painting, writing, or taking long walks by the lake. Perhaps you found satisfaction in working or volunteering at church or in your community. Like a butterfly emerging from the cocoon, stretching its wings to fly, you will need to stretch your thinking to embrace new opportunities and overcome your fears. Let yourself experience again the joy God has for you. Stepping out from what has become a familiar state (being depressed) will take practice and determination.

Chances are many of your relationships will require reconciliation and forgiveness. Depression is hard on relationships with family and friends and within the church family. In my experience, I needed to forgive many people who were not there for me in my depression, accepting that many of them didn't understand the nature of depression. Letting go of bitterness toward others will help your healing process considerably. It will diffuse your anger and feelings of abandonment.

You can begin to reach out to others, taking baby steps if needed. Please hear my heart on this: Isolation can become a lazy habit when you've been depressed for so long. To some extent you will need to push yourself to get out of the house and around other people. Look for opportunities to socialize with others, even if it's just one-on-one to start. Take phone calls if that is something you haven't been able to do up until now. Say "yes" when someone invites you to a social event.

Invite friends or family into your home, but make it easy on yourself by just serving coffee or ordering take-out. Staying in may be easier at first than going out. Remember, the encouragement of fellowship is so much more important than the food on the table!

As you think about getting out of the house, look into taking a class at your community college or join a women's Bible study. It will challenge your mind and offer opportunities to interact with people you may have never met.

You may find that the most difficult area of your recovery will be spiritual. Since depression reaches deep down into the core of who you are—what you value and live for—it has a major impact on your relationship with God. In spiritual recovery we begin to ask ourselves the hard questions: *What is most important in my life? What am I living for? Is my church a safe, supportive place? Who are my spiritual friends?*

In Chapter 4 we heard from several women who

felt abandoned by God in their depression. To them, He appeared to be distant or unresponsive to their prayers. They felt alone and lonely, perhaps even angry. An invisible wall seemed to separate them from the God they had so deeply loved.

How do you know that God understands and hears your cries for help in the midst of depression? By choosing to place your trust in His Word. The book of Psalms, perhaps more than any other book of the Bible, can help you see that others have walked in your shoes—in spiritual and emotional pain—yet were assured of God's love for them. Let's look at two of these psalms together.

> "Those who know your name trust in you, for you, O Lord, have **never abandoned** anyone who searches for you" (Ps. 9:10 NLT, emphasis mine).

> "For the Lord has heard my crying. The Lord has heard my plea; the Lord **will answer** my prayer" (Ps. 6:8b-9 NLT, emphasis mine).

From these verses you can see that God has not abandoned you in your depression. He will answer your prayers as you call on Him even if it's with a weak voice. He reaches down to you in your pain when you cannot find Him.

When I felt my world falling apart, all I could do was figuratively reach a hand heavenward to hang on to Jesus' hand. Little did I realize that He was reaching down to me first as it says in Psalm 18:16: "He reached down from heaven and rescued me; he drew me out of deep waters."

Accepting God's help in the healing process involves obedience on your part. You may want to remain immersed in your pain and negative thinking patterns because they are familiar, but God calls you to step out and embrace health. Medications and counseling therapy will restore enough of your mental and emotional energy to reach out to God and again sense His presence. And finally, as you reach out to spiritual friends and accept their support, you will find many of your relationships restored.

The goal of spiritual recovery is to reconnect with God and accept His love and grace to remedy our issues of guilt, shame, and low self-esteem. We re-establish our personal relationship with God through an act of our will—seeking Him in prayer, reading or listening to His Word, and re-engaging in the life of the church.

God is pleased when you submit your will to Him, even if the feelings take time to follow. As you take small steps of faith, God will meet you more than halfway.

Questions for reflection and discussion:

1) In a practical way, how can we "fix our thoughts on what is true and honorable and right" (Phil. 4:8)? How can relying solely on our feelings get us into trouble?

2) In what ways can you be good to yourself as you are recovering from depression?

3) What steps will you take to restore relationships that have been impacted by your depression?

4) Do you agree that it takes an act of our will to restore our relationship with God?

CHAPTER 19

FACING YOUR FEARS

One of the greatest fears I dealt with in recovery was the fear of falling back into depression. After you've spent months suffering with a dismal mood, lack of energy, and no motivation, it's painful to consider the possibility of relapse. You will want to do everything you can during your recovery to remain emotionally healthy.

Fears are common as you are healing from depression. Many women are concerned if their medications will continue working. If you notice a significant change in your mood, it's important to catch it early so your treatment can be adjusted. Getting help earlier rather than later will assist you in feeling better faster and avoid the risk of a relapse.

Maintaining regular check-ups with your doctor to assess your well-being is important. Your doctor may need to change the dosage of your antidepressant or try a different medication. You may also find that you need to return to your psychotherapist for additional care or increase the frequency of your counseling appointments.

You may also have fears regarding your relationships and how your depression has affected them. I hadn't realized the impact my depression had on my husband until I felt well again. He had taken over many of the household responsibilities, and now I was ready to take them back! We spent time discussing our expectations and arrived at a division of responsibilities that was a win-win for both of us.

There is a certain amount of tentativeness when we think about restoring relationships with our extended family and friends. A sense of awkwardness tends to prevail. First, realize that there is no need to explain yourself. Many people will know you have not felt well for several months and although they may be delighted you are doing better, they are not entitled to a full explanation of what you've been through. Simply tell them you are doing well now and thank them for their concern and well-wishes.

Express thanks to friends who have stood by you through your depression. Tell them how much their support has meant. They are already aware of what you've experienced, so there's no need to explain further. Take time to strengthen your relationship with them.

Co-workers present a more complicated situation. You may not want to talk about your depression at work as it may lead to an unwanted "label." People may treat you differently, including your supervisor if he or she was previously unaware of the reason for your absences. Again, emphasize how well you feel now if anyone asks.

Patience is so important in the process of recovery. Everyone has normal ups and downs; you've just forgotten what they feel like. Don't assume you are falling back into depression if you have a low day. There can be a tendency to over-react and begin to panic that your depression has returned. Do not let that happen! Most likely it's a normal dip in mood and not a relapse.

The healthiest thing you can do is develop a resilient attitude about normal ups and downs. Resiliency involves cultivating a positive mindset. Telling yourself that things are going to be better in a few days will help lift your spirits.

Don't allow yourself to stay mired in gloom. Keep active and focused on your recovery. Positive thoughts will go a long way toward conquering your fears.

Questions for reflection and discussion:

1) What are your greatest fears as you are in the battle or in recovery from depression?

2) If you fear that medication or counseling are not bringing you relief from the symptoms of depression, what additional steps can you take to get help?

3) What does it mean to be "resilient" in the face of depression?

CHAPTER 20

SEARCHING FOR WHAT'S REAL

A curious thing happens when we reach the light at the end of the tunnel of depression. We long to be real. Authentic. Genuine. Slowly, we come to the realization that we cannot go back to wearing a mask, if we've been prone to doing so, pretending that life is okay when it's not.

Many of us are familiar with the beloved children's book, *The Velveteen Rabbit*, by Margery Williams. In the beginning, the Rabbit wants to be like the other toys in the nursery so he will fit in and be accepted. But the wise Skin Horse knows that being yourself, being Real, is of greater value. "It doesn't happen all at once. You become. Generally, by the time you are Real, most of your hair has been loved off, and your eyes drop out and you get loose in the joints and very shabby...Once you are Real you can't become unreal again. It lasts for always."[1]

Like the Velveteen Rabbit, don't we all feel a little droopy and shabby as we are recovering from depression? Maybe you've just started wearing make-up again or exercising to tighten up those muscles not used in awhile. More than anything, though, you want to move back into the world as an authentic person. The journey through depression has a way of drawing out the Real in all of us. It changes us in a way that is at first unsettling, then refreshing and invigorating.

For months I worked at getting my life back on track with God's help. It was difficult to remember what "normal" was like after experiencing depression for so long. The good news was that I didn't have to try and find my way back to the "old me." In fact, I don't think I could go back anyway after all that I had learned and experienced in my depression. I called this my "new normal." It can be your new normal too. Not a discouraging, frantic search for the old and familiar, but a look forward to a full and rewarding life after depression.

How might this "new normal" look for you? You can begin by reflecting on the many things you gave up over the course of your depression. Hobbies, friendships, social relationships, a job, a volunteer commitment, activities, reading, writing—anything that previously made you feel alive and fulfilled. Evaluate each one and determine if it fits with your new way of looking at life.

If old hobbies are no longer appealing, branch out into something new. Search out a new job with fewer hours or more fulfillment. Be willing to make any change that fits with your new normal. It is a process, one of becoming more true to yourself and to how God made you.

We have a God who specializes in creating all things new. He redeems all that has been lost, all the pain and suffering, and uses it for good in our lives. During the recovery process God does not change our core personality, but He gently reshapes how we think about and view the world around us.

I began to search for ways to express my new-found values. I decided to give up some controlling behaviors and be more relaxed in my relationships. I pursued new avenues of creativity, learning to quilt and decorating our home with an eye toward beauty and simplicity. I became more sensitive and compassionate toward the hurting, particularly those who had also suffered with depression.

As part of the healing process, I began to question my faith and to challenge what I believed spiritually. I longed to be part of a church that was filled with Real people—those who had imperfect, messy lives. People who felt the freedom to express their lack of perfection. A church that cried out, "Come as you are." This was the longing of my heart. God, in His grace, guided us to a new church home, one that embraces the less glamorous side of life and loves people where they're at spiritually and emotionally.

As such, the Velveteen Rabbit's story comes to a good but bumpy ending. After the little boy who loved him came down with scarlet fever, the Rabbit was tossed onto the garbage heap to be burned. The germs on his worn coat made him unacceptable. But through the magic of the nursery fairy, the stuffed bunny was trans-formed into a living rabbit. He was given the freedom to laugh and dance and experience life in a much fuller way than he had before. He was Real.

Author Toni Raiten-D'Antonio perhaps said it best when she described this phenomenon of being Real as "living in the moment with the deepest respect for your-self and for others. It is a way of thinking that allows us to express ourselves and experience life…with grace, kindness and integrity."[2]

You, too, can choose to live in the moment. Like the Velveteen Rabbit, laugh, dance and experience life in a way you haven't before. Embrace the Real you and celebrate the unique person God created you to be!

Questions for reflection and discussion:

1) If you are in the healing process, do you find yourself wanting to be Real and authentic with yourself and others? What changes will you make to achieve these goals?

2) What might your post-depression ("new normal") look like?

3) Do you believe God can redeem (use for good) the pain and losses you've experienced with your depression?

CHAPTER 21

UNEXPECTED BLESSINGS

Perhaps by now you've completed your journey through depression. For some, it's been a rough landing. Depression has taught us many lessons and helped us grow in ways we couldn't have if we had not traveled this road. If you have kept a journal, now would be a good time to reread your entries to see how far you've come. In our closing chapter we will look at several blessings that grow out of the experience of depression. They will give you hope that your suffering has not been in vain.

The first blessing is that depression changes women in positive ways. It prompts us to re-evaluate what is most important in life. Attending a funeral will often bring us back to a longing for what's truly important, being reminded that life is short. This might include a renewed focus on relationships, nature, laughter, or beauty. The extraneous is stripped away as things that once were important fade into the background. Depression humbles us, bringing us to our knees where we are more receptive to God's leading.

We come to value people more than things, exchanging selfishness for selflessness. You may have a greater concern for others, particularly those who are suffering with depression. Our heart of compassion grows as God gives us the ability to "comfort those who are in any affliction with the comfort with which we ourselves are comforted by God" (2 Cor. 1:4).

Cheryl, now back to work at the hospital, had this to say about helping others: "I was able to talk to several people who were suffering from depression themselves or had a family member with the illness. I told them how I felt, that there is hope, and about the stigma still surrounding mental illness....I always try to share my experiences and to encourage them. It's nice to have a chance to be used by God to help someone."

Terri, who is in her last semester of graduate school, describes her experience with comforting others as having empathy for them. "You don't feel giving during the depression but you understand people's pain so much better when you feel better. You can give others with depression true understanding."

Women in post-depression also become more sensitive to their own needs. You are more likely to embrace self-care, seeing it not as selfish but as a valuable part of your continued recovery. As women, it's difficult to take time for ourselves. I think you will find that, as you nurture yourself, many other aspects of your life will be less stressful, and you'll enjoy your relationships more.

I think we also learn (the hard way) to pace ourselves in life. That is to say we cannot pack our lives full of activity and expect to remain healthy. I told my counselor I didn't think this restriction was fair. *Why can't I do all the things that others have energy and motivation to do?* He explained wisely that if a person has diabetes they need to take care of themselves in a way that others don't. No, it's not fair, but it's their new reality. Embrace the grace that God provides to cope with your thorn in the flesh.

The second blessing of depression is that it expands our view of God. He uses depression to bring us into a greater understanding of who He is and, therefore, into a deeper relationship with Him. Like Job, we too have experienced confusion, anger, and frustration. From scripture we learn that Job was not delivered from his suffering but gained a new understanding of God's nature: "My ears had heard of you but now my eyes have seen you" (Job 42:5, NIV).

We learn more about life and the character of God through suffering than we do during times of rest. God *is* love, rather than just being loving; therefore, He cannot do anything that is not a reflection of His love. Though God doesn't always provide the answers we seek, He supplies Himself. His purposes in allowing pain and suffering are beyond our understanding. He is compassionate toward us even if we feel He is far away. He is intimately acquainted with our suffering because of His own Son's suffering and death.

The third blessing is that we grow in wisdom and spiritual maturity. The experience of depression is like going back to the Potter's wheel, re-formed to bring God greater glory through our earthly vessel.

Listen to the words of Hosea the prophet: "For I delight in loyalty rather than sacrifice, and in the knowledge of God rather than burnt offerings" (Hos. 6:6). This helps give clarity to our life purpose. It's not about doing things we think are pleasing to God, but about embracing who I am as His beloved child. We can learn to be content being a Mary, sitting faithfully at Jesus' feet, rather than a sacrificial Martha.

In recovery, we grow into a deeper relationship with God. Depression strips us of our ability to control life. It has a way of humbling us into submission to the God who loves us. The good news is that He uses every trial in our life to grow us into Christ-likeness. "For whom he foreknew, He also predestined to become conformed to the image of His Son" (Rom. 8:29). God can even use depression to make us more like Jesus.

Leslie Vernick, author of *Defeating Depression*, understood this when she wrote, "Wanting what God wants and a desire to be made willing are important parts of becoming more like Christ, even in the midst of great suffering."[1]

Depression gives us the ability to look at life in a new way. We are given fresh vision—new eyes to see God, other people, and ourselves. Like a near-death experience, we come to value life more than we did before. We begin to look to God with eyes of faith and trust. We see others with eyes of compassion, and we see ourselves with greater understanding and acceptance.

Bless you, dear one, as you continue on your journey. Hold fast to hope and to the God who loves you passionately. He has promised to never leave you or forsake you in the storms of life. He is the Light that dispels the darkness. You can trust in Him.

Questions for reflection and discussion:

1) In what ways have you experienced personal growth as a result of your depression?

2) How can you see God using you to minister to others, to "comfort those who are in any affliction with the comfort with which we are comforted by God"? Do you sense that God is calling you to share your story with other women experiencing depression?

3) Read over the Bible verses listed in "Encouragement From the Scriptures." Highlight or put a star by the verses that mean the most to you. You may even want to write these scriptures on note cards for easy reference. Encourage yourself with these passages of scripture when you are feeling down.

A LETTER TO HUSBANDS

Over the years, my husband and I enjoyed watching our children's sporting events. From playing soccer and T-ball in Kindergarten, to our son's high school football team winning the state championship his senior year, we were right there to cheer them on.

I especially remember their first year of soccer. Though fun to watch, there was little teamwork and more of a humorous "every-man-for-himself" attitude. Then, as they got a little older, it was more common to see one child kick the ball all the way down the field rather than pass it off to a teammate. Playing this way caused the rest of the team to feel left out.

By the time they reached middle and high school, there was a real sense of teamwork and the kids understood that winning the game was more about pulling together and less about being a lone ranger.

Likewise, family and friends must pull together as a team to support a loved one in their battle against depression. Because teamwork is so important, I've included this chapter to address the questions and concerns of spouses. While we don't often consider the people surrounding a depressed person, they are just as affected, though in different ways. As mentioned before, depression is isolating, but it's also isolating for those in a supportive role.

To continue the team metaphor, it's never good to go it alone, to be the one carrying the ball downfield by yourself. It's too discouraging. Instead, you need to build a strong support network. It will give you the resilience to stay positive and have the energy to care for your wife. Team members can include extended family, friends, neighbors, pastors, therapists, and medical professionals. All of these can work together to support you and promote healing in your spouse.

What are some of the feelings husbands experience when their wife struggles with depression? You may find that your marriage passes through several emotional stages. Before the depression is identified, you may feel frustrated that your wife has become lethargic, pessimistic, and anti-social. You are confused by the changes you see in her, and angry that she doesn't just "snap out of it." Communication becomes tense, and irritability with each other is common.

As the depression progresses, you may begin feeling lonely, sad, and unloved as your wife pulls back from the relationship. Communication becomes an everyday challenge as one withdraws and one pursues. You may take on extra tasks around the house but receive little appreciation.

You find yourself alternating between anger and resentment, experiencing guilt for feeling the way you do. Finally, the worry and exhaustion take their toll and you will either withdraw and avoid your wife or go into overdrive to help her while ignoring your own needs. Neither is good or healthy.

So what is a husband to do to avoid being sucked into the downward spiral of his wife's depression? The first and most important thing is to care for yourself. Try to stick to your usual routine and activities as much as possible to maintain a sense of normalcy.

If you usually work out in the mornings or play basketball one evening a week with the guys, stay with it! Exercise will also reduce the stress you feel while caring for your spouse.

Don't be afraid to share your feelings at the risk of upsetting your wife. Remember, your thoughts and feelings are just as important as hers.

Secondly, keep the lines of communication open as much as possible. Remember the team concept? Help your wife understand that you are not the opponent. You are part of her team and on her side. In fact, you're her biggest cheerleader.

Don't take your spouse's words or actions personally or become defensive. Instead, draw your wife out with gentle questions of concern. Depressed people are reluctant to share their feelings because they are afraid to burden other people and are ashamed of how they think and feel. Move out of the problem-solving mode— where men are most comfortable—into a sympathizing role. Let her know how much you love her even when she feels unlovable.

Third, be aware that depressed people will often reject any help that is offered them. They already feel helpless and inferior, so to rely on someone else for assistance adds insult to injury. Deep down, your wife wants help but is too ashamed to ask. Continue to offer support even if it isn't accepted right away, keeping in mind that normal routines and responsibilities are overwhelming to her.

If you can help shoulder the burden of housecleaning, cooking and laundry, she will feel less pressure to perform. Whenever you can enlist her to work on things as a couple, it will help your wife feel supported and useful.

Marriages are strained when one spouse struggles with depression. Just as muscles grow stronger when they are tested, so your marriage will be strengthened as you walk through difficult times together. Through marriage vows, couples promise to love one another in good times and bad, in sickness and in health, as long as they are on this earth.

Your part in the relationship is to support your wife with unconditional love and full acceptance. It may not seem apparent, but she truly values you more than you know.

HOPE

You reached down and pulled me out
Of this mire and clay, and painful doubt.
Hope was lost but now is found.
Your tender voice, how sweet the sound.

Once I lived in darkness, gray.
I thought that You had gone away
And left me to my suffering,
With tears my only offering.

King David understood my loss,
The Psalms he wrote, emotions tossed
Upon his pillow, night after night.
But he would not give up the fight

I fought, too, when all looked bleak.
God gave me strength, I was so weak.
He set me on a firm foundation;
"All for love," His explanation

Hope came knocking at my door today.
I will not fear, God makes a way.
His light will shine, when all seems lost.
I am free, Christ paid the cost.

Encouragement from the Scriptures*

*the following are taken from the New Living Translation (NLT) unless otherwise noted

Ps. 9:9-10 "The Lord is a shelter for the oppressed, a refuge in times of trouble. Those who know your name trust in you, for you, O Lord, have never abandoned anyone who searches for you"

Ps. 147:3 "He heals the brokenhearted, binding up their wounds"

Is. 40:29 "He gives power to those who are tired and worn out; He offers strength to the weak"

Ps. 18:16,18-19 "He reached down from on high and took hold of me; He drew me out of deep waters....the Lord was my support. He brought me out into a spacious place; He rescued me because he delighted in me" (NIV)

Jer. 30:17 "I will give you back your health and heal your wounds, says the Lord"

Ps. 9:12b "He does not ignore those who cry to Him for help"

Ps. 16:8 "I know the Lord is always with me. I will not be shaken, for He is right beside me"

Rom. 15:13 "So I pray that God, who gives you hope, will keep you happy and full of peace as you believe in Him. May you overflow with hope through the power of the Holy Spirit"

Ps. 6:8b-9 "For the Lord has heard my crying. The Lord has heard my plea; the Lord will answer my prayer"

Ps. 139:7,10 "I can never escape from your Spirit! I can never get away from your presence....your hand will guide me and your strength will support me"

Ps. 22:24 "For He has not ignored the suffering of the needy. He has not turned and walked away. He has listened to their cries for help"

Ps. 46:1 "God is our refuge and strength, always ready to help in times of trouble"

Ps. 18:5-6 "The grave wrapped its ropes around me; death itself stared me in the face. But in my distress I cried out to the Lord; yes, I prayed to my God for help. He heard me from His sanctuary; my cry reached His ears"

Jer. 33:6 "Behold, I will bring (them) health and healing, and I will heal them; and I will reveal to them an abundance of peace and truth" (NASB)

For Additional Information

General information on depression:

National Institute of Mental Health (NIMH), 6001
Executive Blvd. Room 8184, MSC 9663, Bethesda,
MD 20892-9663. Toll free: (866) 615-6464.
http://www.nimh.nih.gov/
A number of free publications pertaining to mental
health issues are available for order on their website.
Click on the Health Info tab, then on Publications.

National Alliance for the Mentally Ill (NAMI),
Colonial Place Three, 2107 Wilson Blvd. Suite 300,
Arlington, VA 22201-3042. Toll-Free: (800) 950-6264.
http://www.nami.org/

National Mental Health Association 2001 N.
Beauregard St. 12th Floor, Alexandria, VA 22311
Toll-Free: (800) 969-6642.
http://www.nmha.org/

American Psychiatric Association 1400 K St., NW
Washington, DC 20005
Toll-Free: (888) 357-7924. http://www.psych.org/

American Psychological Association's Help Center
750 First St. NE, Washington, DC 20002 Toll-Free:
(800) 374-2721. http://www.apahelpcenter.org

Women and Depression
www.psycom.net/depression.central.women

The National Women's Health Information Center
www.womenshealth.gov

Christian Depression Pages
www.Christian-depression.org

Dysthymia

U.S. National Library of Medicine: PubMed Health
www.ncbi.nlm.nih.gov/pubmedhealth/PMH0001916

Mayo Clinic
www.mayoclinic.com/health/dysthymia/DS01111

WebMD www.webmd.com/depression/guide/
chronic-depression-dysthymia

Seasonal Affective Disorder (SAD)

Mayo Clinic www.mayoclinic.com/health/
seasonal-affective-disorder/DS00195

National Institutes of Health—Medline Plus
www.nlm.nih.gov/medlineplus/seasonalaffectivedisor-
der.html

WebMD www.webmd.com/depression/guide/
seasonal-affective-disorder

Light Therapy

Full Spectrum Solutions
www.fullspectrumsolutions.com

Verilux www.verilux.com

Postpartum Depression:

Depression After Delivery
Toll free: (800) 944-4773.
http://www.depressionafterdelivery.com/

Postpartum Support International
(631) 422-2255. www.postpartum.net/

Bipolar Disorder:

Depression and Bipolar Support Alliance (DBSA), 730 N. Franklin St., Suite 501, Chicago, IL 60654-7225. Toll free: (800) 826-3632. www.dbsalliance.org

U.S. National Library of Medicine: PubMed Health www.ncbi.nlm.nih.gov/pubmedhealth/PMH0001924/

Mayo Clinic www.mayoclinic.com/health/bipolar-disorder/

WebMD www.webmd.com/bipolar-disorder

Suggested Reading

Depression: A Woman Doctor's Guide by Jane S. Ferber, M.D. with Suzanne LeVert (2000)

Why Do I Feel This Way? by Brenda Poinsett (1996)

New Light on Depression by David Biebel, D. Min. and Harold G. Koenig, M.D. (2004)

Understanding Depression by J. Raymond DePaulo Jr., M.D. (2002)

Spirit-Controlled Temperament by Tim LaHaye (1994)

Come As You Are by Betty Southard and Marita Littauer (1999)

Defeating Depression by Leslie Vernick (2005)

When Someone You Love is Depressed by Laura Epstein Rosen, Ph.D. and Xavier Francisco Amador, Ph.D. (1996)

Crying for the Light: Bible Readings and Reflections for Living with Depression by Veronica Zundel (2009)

The Dark Night of the Soul by Gerald G. May, M.D. (2004)

Depression: A Stubborn Darkness by Edward T. Welch, M. Div., Ph.D. (2004)

Winter Blues by Norman E. Rosenthal, M.D. (1998)

Positive Options For Seasonal Affective Disorder by Fiona Marshall and Peter Cheevers (2003)

A Woman's Guide to Overcoming Depression by Archibald Hart and Catherine Hart Weber (2007)

Living Beyond Postpartum Depression by Jerusha Clark (2010)

Happiness is a Choice, updated edition, by Frank Minirth, M.D. and Paul Meier, M.D. (2007)

The Velveteen Principles: A Guide to Becoming Real by Toni Raiten-D'Antonio (2004)

Notes

Chapter 2

[1] Clayton L. Thomas, Editor, Taber's Cyclopedic Medical Dictionary, 18th ed. (Philadelphia: F.A. Davis Co., 1993), 512.

[2] Ibid, 41

[3] Brenda Poinsett, *Why Do I Feel This Way?* (Colorado Springs, CO: Navpress, 1996), 15.

[4] Wikipedia.org, accessed Feb. 2010 (Elisabeth Kubler-Ross).

Chapter 6

[1] Psychiatric Association Diagnostic and Statistical Manual of Mental Disorders, 4th ed., 1994.

Chapter 7

[1] Taber's Medical Dictionary, 591.

[2] Ibid, 586, 1949.

Chapter 8

[1] Jane S. Ferber, M.D. with Suzanne LeVert, *Depression: A Woman Doctor's Guide* (New York: Kensington Publishing Corp., 2000), 56.

[2] David Biebel, D. Min. and Harold G. Koenig, M.D., *New Light on Depression* (Grand Rapids, MI: Zondervan, 2004), 46.

Chapter 9

[1] American College of Obstetricians and Gynecologists, patient education pamphlet, Jan. 2009.

[2] Ibid.

Chapter 10

[1] Biebel and Koenig, 47.

[2] J. Raymond DePaulo Jr., M.D. *Understanding Depression*. (Hoboken, NJ: John Wiley and Sons, Inc., 2002), 28-29.

Chapter 11

[1] Tim LaHaye, *Spirit-Controlled Temperament* (Wheaton, IL: Tyndale House Publishers, Inc., 1994), 10.

[2] Betty Southard and Marita Littauer, *Come As You Are* (Minneapolis, MN: Bethany House Publishers, 1999), 136-137.

Chapter 16

[1] J. Raymond DePaulo Jr., M.D., 261.

[2] Paul David Tripp, *Lost in the Middle* (Wapwallopen, PA: Shepherd Press, 2004), 60.

Chapter 17

[1] Biebel and Koenig, 67.

[2] Webster's New World College Dictionary, 4th ed., 2000.

[3] Biebel and Koenig, 88.

Chapter 20

[1] Margery Williams, *The Velveteen Rabbit* (Random House Inc., 1985).

[2] Toni Raiten-D'Antonio, *The Velveteen Principles: A Guide to Becoming Real* (Deerfield Beach, FL: Health Communications, Inc., 2004), 13.

Chapter 21

[1] Leslie Vernick, *Defeating Depression* (Eugene, OR: Harvest House Publishers, 2005), 85.

CPSIA information can be obtained
at www.ICGtesting.com
Printed in the USA
FFOW04n1501220415
12861FF